structure subject to a demolition order. At Lutyens' suggestion, negotiations for its purchase were entered into with its owner, a local auctioneer called Charles Butcher, and were concluded in June 1910 for the sum of £75. The need to integrate this building into the scheme was the deciding factor in the form that the house would take. The components of the Old House at Home were carefully numbered and the building was then dismantled. The following year it was re-erected at Dixter, where the accommodation it provided included the principal bedroom, now the Yeoman's Hall, flanked by a dressing room and bathroom, with a further bedroom and the night nursery upstairs. In all aspects of the restoration, Lloyd was keen to ensure that nothing was faked: 'The spirit in which the work has been done may be summed up by saying that nothing has been done without authority, nothing has been done from imagination; there has been no forgery' (from an unpublished memorandum by Nathaniel Lloyd, c. 1913).

Work proceeded somewhat erratically, as Lutyens was extremely busy on other jobs, including a visit to South Africa, and sometimes dilatory in supplying the necessary drawings. The surviving correspondence between Lloyd and Lutyens indicates that Lloyd was an impatient client who was not inclined to be fobbed off with the frequent and charmingly expressed excuses offered by Lutyens and his unfortunate chief assistant Albert Thomas. Regrettably the later correspondence from summer 1911 is lost, but work was concluded by late 1912. The following year, Great Dixter became the subject of

The Old House at Home, Benenden, now incorporated as the Yeoman's Hall

The Solar in use as a hospital

an illustrated article in Country Life and the house has changed little since that time, apart from the loss of some of its contents in 1994 caused by a sale.

Nathaniel Lloyd was so entranced by the pleasures of building and building history that, with characteristic energy, he trained himself in architectural drawing and developed a small practice as an architect. His chief work was the careful restoration of Higham, a fine 16th and 17th-century house in Northiam, where he undid unsympathetic alterations of the 19th century, proving himself an apt pupil of Lutyens. He also designed new cottages in Northiam and a substantial country house at Ewhurst called Prawles. Most importantly, however, his studies of historic buildings led to much writing, including the publication (largely illustrated from his own photographs) of two monographs that have remained standard works to the present day and are still in print, A History of English Brickwork (first published 1925) and A History of the English House (1931).

Great Dixter was originally run with a staff of about five, including a chauffeur, a cook, two housemaids and a nursery maid, who had to look after Mr and Mrs Lloyd and their six children. Outside staff included nine gardeners. During the First World War the house became a hospital and in 1940 it housed evacuee children who used the Great Hall as a dormitory. Nathaniel died in 1933, and the estate of some 450 acres including Little Dixter, which had been purchased at an early stage, was run by his formidable widow Daisy until her death in 1972. Since then the estate has been divided and the house and gardens are now the property of the gardening writer Christopher Lloyd and his niece Olivia Eller.

The Exterior

As you face the entrance side of Great Dixter, the porch and everything to the right is 15th or early 16th-century, while the left hand side of the house, containing service quarters below and bedrooms above, is by Edwin Lutyens. The extraordinary sweep of the tiled roof, particularly when seen from the upper garden, punctuated by tall chimneys and small dormer windows, is the most dramatic element of Lutyens' otherwise self-effacing work at Great Dixter. Following the path to the right, the huge chimney breast on the end wall of the house was a substitution by Lutyens for the miserable small flues then serving the Parlour and Solar. The ground on the garden side of the house falls away quite steeply, so a terrace was built where additions to the south side of the Great Hall were destroyed, and the reconstructed house from Benenden was erected on a high brick base (containing the Billiard Room). As you begin to walk along the Long Border, look back at the east side of the house. On the right on the first floor is a small window on a different level from all the others. This was a characteristic touch of Lutyens' and is a floor level window in the Day Nursery. He called it the Crawling Window. Few great architects would have bothered to ensure that the smallest inhabitant, unable to reach a conventional window sill, could also see out. The doorway (now blocked) in the end of the Benenden house is original.

Guide to the Rooms – Great Hall

This is virtually in the state in which it was left at the completion of the restoration in 1911. Despite major alterations made about 1595, since removed, the principal medieval features of the hall have remained relatively intact. It is one of the largest surviving timber-framed halls in the country (measuring 40 feet by 25 feet and 31 feet high – 12.2m by 7.6m and 9.5m high) and the fine roof has hammerbeams strengthened with a tiebeam. This is supported by two tie braces cut from a single oak tree branch containing a woodpecker's nest, which was thus cut in

two (visible on the western or dais side). The fine armorial shields on the hammerbeams depict the arms of the Etchinghams, the Dalyn-grigges and the Gaynesfords and suggest an approximate building date of between 1440 and 1454. The house was built for Richard Wakehurst (died 1454), his wife (through whom he acquired the estate) was Elizabeth Etchingham and his brother-in-law was John Gaynesford. The Dalyngrigges of nearby Bodiam Castle intermarried with the Etchinghams in the 14th and 15th centuries.

Originally the hall was heated by an open fire in the centre of the floor, like the surviving example at Penshurst Place, Kent. The smoke found its way out through windows, not glazed then but closed with wooden shutters, or through a hole in the roof capped by a long-vanished louvre. The roof beams are still blackened as a result. The floor would have been beaten earth, strewn with rushes. At the upper end was a dais, about 15 inches high (0.4m), and the

The Great Hall

A Guide to
Great Dixter

Christopher Lloyd
Charles Hind

A Guide to
Great Dixter

First published in 1995 by Angel Design

Revised 1999

ISBN 0 9525471 0 4

Text © Christopher Lloyd and Charles Hind, 1999

Old photographs of Great Dixter © Great Dixter, 1999

Photography: Jonathan Buckley (courtesy of IPC Magazines) – page 12, page 13, page 15, page 16 and 17; Fergus Garrett – page 11; Jerry Harpur – page 9, page 10, back cover; Christopher Lloyd – inside front cover, page 14; David Sellman – page 4/5, page 6, page 7; Steve Wooster – front cover, inside back cover.

Angel Design, Sea View, Queen's Road, Lydd, Romney Marsh, Kent TN29 9DB

A History of Great Dixter – Charles Hind

The first glimpse of Great Dixter, its great tiled and timbered bulk reclining comfortably on the gentle slope of the hill, suggests that here is a building of great antiquity, surely completed by the end of the Middle Ages, and as much a part of the history of the Sussex Weald as Bodiam Castle or Northiam Church. Appearances are deceptive, however, and the present Great Dixter is actually three houses, one built here in the mid-15th century with slightly later additions, the second a yeoman's house from Benenden, across the border in Kent, built in the early 16th century and moved here in 1910, and the third combines the two with additional accommodation, completed in 1912. It was at this time that the house, hitherto called merely Dixter, was renamed Great Dixter, to distinguish it from Little Dixter next door.

The Manor of Dixter

Dixter is first recorded in 1220, but the earliest surviving part of the house, the Great Hall, dates probably from the 1450s. Most of the owners of the manor are known from 1340, when it was one Hamo at Gate, whose feudal obligation to the king was to supply one man-at-arms when required. His property at 'Dicksterve' was valued at 40 shillings. Haro's daughter Joan married Robert de Etchingham and after their deaths, the property passed to Robert's younger brother Richard and his descendants, one of whom, another Robert de Etchingham, was in possession by 1411. Robert's daughter Elizabeth married Richard Wakehurst, who built the present house before his death in 1454. Although Wakehurst had two daughters, by the marriage settlement the estate returned to the de Etchinghams on his widow's death, and from them it passed to Andrew Windsor, 1st Lord Windsor. The Windsors retained it until 1595, when they sold it to John Glydd. In 1574 the 3rd Lord Windsor died in Venice, where a monument to his memory was erected in the church of SS Giovanni e Paolo. Its inscription mentions his ownership of Dixter, although the house had been let since 1558 to the Harrison family.

From Glydd, the house passed by descent to the Gott family, who sold Dixter in 1797 to George Springett (died 1819) for £2,550. He was a bachelor, as was his nephew and heir, another George Springett (died 1864), so in due course the house was inherited by the latter's niece Sarah Elizabeth Springett (1839–1928), who married a Dr Pout, but understandably perhaps, she retained her maiden name. She never lived at Dixter, using it only for the shooting but let the house until she sold it to Nathaniel Lloyd in 1910. It had been on the market for ten years advertised as an agricultural property with farmhouse attached.

The Lloyd Family and the Restoration of the House

Nathaniel Lloyd was born in 1867 to a comfortably-off middle-class family in Manchester. His maternal grandfather owned a department store in Glasgow. Lloyd's early business career included managing the advertising and printing of the Mazzawattee Tea Co. but in 1893 he founded his own colour printing firm. This became so successful that by 1909 he was able to retire and devote himself to his passions for shooting and golf. He was also keenly interested in antique furniture, at this stage principally Georgian, but

Lutyens' building work in progress

A painting of Dixter before Lutyens started work

he had also acquired a number of French pieces. When furnishing Great Dixter, his view developed that good furniture of any period could live in harmony and in due course the house contained a rich mixture of pieces ranging from 15th-century French and 16th-century Italian to English of all periods from medieval to early 19th-century.

In 1905 Nathaniel married Daisy Field, daughter of a successful London solicitor Basil Field, and the couple leased a late 19th-century house in Rye, where Nathaniel could play golf at weekends. When he retired from business in 1909 Nathaniel began looking for an old house to buy, and the purchase of Dixter and its immediate grounds and farm buildings was agreed in May 1910, for the sum of £6,000.

Lloyd's first requirement was an architect and he asked two, Sir Ernest George, R.A., and a former pupil of his, Edwin Lutyens, to submit outline schemes for restoring and enlarging the house. George was a senior and respected figure in the architectural profession, who had made his name and fortune building substantial country houses in the Jacobean style and town houses on the Cadogan and Grosvenor Estates in London. Although his design for Dixter is lost, a description of it by George's son Allen, a close friend of Lloyd's, indicates that it would have involved a drastic restoration of the existing house and substantial additions that would have made Dixter a

large and unremarkable, essentially Victorian country house.

Edwin Lutyens had spent only six months in George's office before setting up his own practice in 1889 at the age of 20. He made his name with a series of brilliant country house designs, often enlarging or adapting existing buildings and always showing a remarkable sympathy for the convincing use of local materials and building traditions. Through his association with the gardener and designer Gertrude Jekyll, he also acquired a reputation for welding houses and gardens together and indeed popularising a completely new approach to English gardens. Despite this and contrary to popular legend, Miss Jekyll had nothing whatever to do with Dixter, for which Lutyens alone was responsible. Lutyens' original sketches have survived and show a building quite unlike the present house, but were sufficient to convince Lloyd instantly that he would be the right choice. Sir Ernest George, to his chagrin, was paid off and Lutyens began detailed drawings.

Lloyd was keen that the restoration and enlargement of Great Dixter should reflect local traditions and so he and Lutyens motored round the area examining old buildings. At Benenden, some nine miles away from Northiam, they saw the derelict remains of an early 16th-century timber house called the Old House at Home, the chimney of which had collapsed, rendering the mortice holes for its supports can still be seen in the posts at the end of the wall. Here the lord of the manor, his family and favoured guests would have eaten their meals. Behind them is the door to the parlour and on the left is the door to the stairs leading up to the solar, parlour and solar being the private rooms of the family. At the other end of the hall was a screen, perhaps with a gallery over it, with what was called a screens passage behind it, into which the front door opened. The screen's position is marked by the change from moulded to unmoulded beam in the south wall. The doorways in the east or end wall of the hall led to the buttery and kitchens, long since vanished.

About 1595 the hall was subdivided with two floors, the ground floor becoming two rooms with a great brick chimney built between them. By the late 16th century, great halls were going out of fashion in lesser houses and many were divided up to create smaller, more comfortable and more easily heated rooms. The bay windows

were destroyed and further rooms on two floors were added against the south wall. Probably in the late 17th century, the porch was sealed up and made into a room (by 1910 it was a larder) and a new front door inserted beside it. The remaining windows not already blocked up were converted into casements at the same time. This division of the interior lasted until 1910, when the house was bought by Nathaniel Lloyd and his architect Edwin Lutyens opened it all up again. The central chimney stack was carefully dismantled and moved to the east end, where Lutyens made no attempt to recreate the lost screen and instead constructed a wind porch to protect the hall from the draughts of the front door. Beneath late 16th-century plasterwork several of the original windows survived intact and the rest were reinstated. The Lloyds used the hall daily as their dining and living room until the Second World War. Although they were keen to preserve all the old structure, the Lloyds were not prepared to be uncomfortable and modern amenities were installed from the first, including central heating and electricity, which ran off a generator. The hanging lights are those originally installed in 1911 and the radiators are concealed beneath old oak chests adapted for the purpose, as in many of the other rooms.

Principal contents:
A late 15th-century lectern from SW France. An oak refectory table (c. 1600), with half rosettes carved on the frieze facing into the room. The side facing the wall was left plain. Several late 17th-century oak or walnut high backed chairs.
An English oak court cupboard bearing the initials of its first owners: IS ES 1670.
An oak refectory table designed and made by Nathaniel Lloyd and his son Patrick in 1932.

Parlour
When the Parlour is in use by Mr Lloyd, the Yeoman's Hall will be opened instead.
In medieval times the parlour was one of the private rooms of the family to which they could retreat from the rather public Great Hall. It was originally equipped with a stone fireplace similar to the surviving one upstairs in the Solar, but this was so mutilated and damaged by 1910 that

The Parlour

Lutyens replaced it with the broad hearth and the reused timber beam we see today. The room was originally about a third longer, but the late 16th-century partition was left by Lutyens and the room beyond became an office (not open to the public). Carved on a beam above the piano can be seen the inscription: JOHN HARRISON DWELT ATT DIXTERN XXXVI YERS AN VI MONTHES. CAME YE FERST OF ELISA-BETHE RAIN. Harrison was a tenant who occupied the house from 1558 until 1595, when the house was sold to John Glydd, who was responsible for the subdivision of the Great Hall. Until 1910 the beam and its inscription were hidden by a later plaster ceiling.

When the Lloyds moved to Dixter, Daisy Lloyd used the Parlour as her writing room. She was a skilled needlewoman and several examples of her embroidery can be seen here, including the fine armchair near the fireplace. Most of the embroidery in the house is by Daisy or her children, and it was she who collected the samplers that hang in several rooms. She generally worked her embroidery by the south window in the

Great Hall. The outer pairs of windows here in the Parlour were the only 15th-century ones to survive intact beneath later plasterwork and were used as the model for the restoration of those in the Great Hall.

Principal contents:

The fireback of local Sussex iron bears the arms of King Charles II.

Early 18th-century English walnut bureau with mirrored doors.

Early 18th-century English walnut dining chair.

George II wing chair upholstered with embroidery by Daisy Lloyd and her sons Patrick and Christopher. Their respective contributions are initialled and dated.

Pair of late 18th-century elbow chairs after a design by Thomas Hepplewhite.

Early 19th-century card table in mahogany and satinwood. This once belonged to Henry Crabb Robinson (1775–1867), a journalist, lawyer and, in his day, a famous conversationalist. It was inherited from the Field family by Daisy Lloyd.

A simple oak writing table, one of several of a similar design in the house probably by Lutyens.

Solar

By 1910, the original staircase to the solar had long since disappeared, and Lutyens replaced a plain 19th-century staircase with the present oak one. The cellar door is the only original one in the house and was found in the moat. It was used as a model for others. A portrait engraving of Lutyens hangs here, as does a fine embroidered carpet, made by Letitia, the Lloyds' only daughter. Upstairs by the Solar door hangs a rubbing of the brass memorial to Sir William de Etchingham (died 1412) in Etchingham Church. He was a relative of the Etchinghams who owned Great Dixter in the 15th century.

The Solar was the principal private apartment of the medieval house. The fireplace dates from the late 15th century and its spandrels bear the devices of the Lewknors of Bodiam (a hawk's lure) and the antlered head of the Windsors, who inherited Dixter about the time the fireplace was installed. The Solar was divided into three rooms by John Glydd and reconstituted by the Lloyds. The Squint into the Great Hall was a typical feature of such houses

The Solar

but in fact was inserted by Lutyens. The window at the south end contains a 16th-century painted glass panel copied after a print of 1518 by Albrecht Dürer. When Nathaniel Lloyd turned to architecture, he used the north end as his office, working at the draughtsman's table. A photograph on the bookcase to the left shows him at work.

Principal contents:

Early 18th-century Dutch longcase clock by Obbe Hendricks of Harlingen, surmounted by figures of Atlas flanked by two dancing maidens. English walnut card table (*c.* 1730), with a later detachable top transforming it into a tea table. Mid-18th century English mahogany draughtsman's table.
Mid-18th century 'Chippendale' serpentine fronted commode or chest of drawers.
Oak standard lamp designed by Nathaniel Lloyd. Modern armchair, table, waste paper bin and coffee table made by Rupert Williamson of oak inlaid with ebony.
The remaining furniture is principally English and 18th-century.

The Yeoman's Hall when in use as a bedroom

The following rooms are only open to the public when not in use by Mr Lloyd

Waiting Hall

This part of the house is entirely the work of Lutyens. Through the arch on the left can be seen the secondary staircase with its oak lattice panels, which Lutyens copied from a 16th-century example at Hushheath Manor, near Staplehurst, Kent. The door beneath the main staircase conceals steps that lead down to a billiard room.

Principal contents:

17th-century oak court cupboard.
Late 17th-century panel of printed linen (over the staircase), much decayed by exposure to light.
Early 18th-century walnut and marquetry long-case clock by Roger Fenton.
18th-century pewter colander

Dressing Room

This and the Yeoman's Hall next door are in the early 16th-century house brought from Benenden.

Principal contents:

Mid-18th century commode or chest of drawers, its top drawer fitted with a writing slope and dressing table accoutrements.
20th-century bed in an early 18th-century manner.

Yeoman's Hall

Originally this served as Mr and Mrs Lloyd's bedroom and it was illustrated as such in the article on Great Dixter published by Country Life in 1913. A high bed built up on a panelled dais, copied after a 16th-century example in the Palazzo Davanzati, Florence, stood against the far wall. Since the last war, the room has served as a summer sitting room.

As built at Benenden, this house was occupied by a yeoman farmer and was therefore far less grand than Great Dixter, although built upon similar lines. The central room served as a hall, with subsidiary rooms at each end. The hall never boasted a screen, but the master sat at the top end, where the crenellated beam that crosses the hall was returned two feet into the room to provide shelter from the draughts through the neighbouring doorway. Again there would have been a central hearth; the present fireplace is by Lutyens. In the course of dismantling the building, some of the original upright window bars were uncovered. The windows on the left were sealed with oak boards, as they back onto the Lutyens additions, while those on the right were glazed.

Principal Contents:

Late 17th-century oak gateleg table.
Early 18th-century walnut secretaire cabinet.
Early 18th-century walnut tallboy.
Modern standard lamp by Rupert Williamson.

From here, visitors are requested to retrace their steps to the front door.

BIBLIOGRAPHY

J.E. Ray: 'Dixter, Northiam. A Fifteenth Century Timber Manor House', Sussex Archaeological Society Collections, vol. lii (1909).
Lawrence Weaver: 'Great Dixter, Sussex', Country Life, vol. xxxiii, no. 835, January, 1913, pp. 18–26.
Quentin Lloyd: A Guide to Great Dixter (Northiam, c. 1960).
Charles Hind: 'Great Dixter, Sussex', Country Life, vol. clxxxix, no. 44, November 2nd, 1995, pp. 50–55.
Unpublished letters, manuscripts and drawings at Great Dixter.

The Gardens at Great Dixter – Christopher Lloyd

One of the pleasant features about the gardens is that they lie all around the house. Make a circuit of the gardens and you have made a circuit of the house exterior. Each has good views of the other.

Apart from a couple of mixed orchards and a scattering of trees there were no gardens here when my parents arrived on the scene in 1910. Of the trees a few survive: three pears, including a Williams, still cropping well; the bay laurel near to the front path; a black fig, commonly planted in Northiam and a yew tree, which my father cut back and retrained as a topiary specimen. The apparent antiquity of the yew hedges is spurious. All, as well as the topiary, in which my father was particularly interested, were planted in 1912 or later.

Topiary

The yew topiary lends a particular atmosphere to several parts of the garden. There was more of it in my father's time. It has a presence, especially when shadows are long and it appears to inhabit, rather than grow. It needs clipping only once a year. If done in August, it will retain its sharp outlines right through to the end of the following May. However, although we mechanised the operation soon after the last war, we seldom achieve this objective and are pleased if this pro-longed task is completed by November. Yew grows much faster than people imagine, if the ground is well prepared and the plants are fed.

Design

Most of the garden design was by Lutyens; it always seems fluid, never stodgy. Thus, yew hedges are sometimes curved, making a change from straight lines. He often used tiles in a decorative (though functional) manner. Thus, a chicken house with rotten walls, was turned into an open sided loggia, supported by laminated tile pillars. In so far as possible, Lutyens incorporated farm buildings into his design, turning them to other uses. Four brick cattle drinking tanks

Aster hedges linking the peacock topiary pieces

were retained; we have now filled these in and planted them.

The paving is of York sandstone. This had comprised London's pavements, but when ripped up to be replaced by tarmac, the stone became available for garden use. Lichens grow on it, making their own patterns, particularly noticeable at their 'flowering', in April. But the stone is slippery when wet.

My father was responsible for the design and making of the Sunk Garden, originally lawn, then dug up for vegetables during the First World War, after which my father said 'Now we can play'. The spoil was removed to fill in a pond on the other side of the garden.

Oast House and Barn

The barn, with its long, tiled roof reaching quite near to ground level, on the garden side, is characteristic of this part of the Weald. It is supposed to be contemporary with Dixter itself, but the structure within is unimpressive. The oast house, with its three kilns, was built around 1890, and hops from the nearby hop garden were dried in it up to 1939. The delicious smell as they steamed, is one of my most nostalgic

Wild flowers follow the daffodils

memories. The oast house cowls turn with the wind so as always to have their backs to it, thereby preventing the smoke and steam from blowing back into the kiln.

The Meadow Areas

Your first sight, on entering the front gate, is of two areas of rough grass, either side of the path to the house. These, and a number of other, similar areas, scattered through the garden, bear witness to my mother's love of this kind of meadow gardening. They are not just plots of grass that we gave up mowing for lack of labour, but were intended from the first.

They contain a rich assortment of plants that enjoy growing in turf and the grass is not cut until all its contents have completed ripening and shedding their seed. Much of this is native material that needed no introduction. The poorer the soil, the richer the tapestry that can be created. If the soil is fertile, a few coarse elements like cow parsley, yorkshire fog, nettles and docks, will dominate and smother all else.

The grass is cut twice (August and late autumn) and all is removed and composted. Orchids native to the Weald are a particular

Barn Garden – strong foliage combination in a mixed planting

success; early purples, green winged, twayblade and spotted (*Dactylorhiza fuchsii*). It is a sanctuary for them, since changed farming and woodland practices have eliminated most of their natural habitats.

My mother used to raise wild daffodils (*Narcissus pseudonarcissus*) and snakeshead fritillaries (*Fritillaria meleagris*) from seed, prick out the seedlings and eventually plant them out. They have been a notable success. Exotics like the North American bulb, *Camassia quamash*, have also thrived. Their spikes of starry blue flowers are a feature alongside the front path in May. We keep experimenting with other ingredients, looking for those that will take care of themselves, once given a start.

Man-made daffodil hybrids are nearly all located in the orchard, on the south side of the house. They are not so thickly planted as to exclude crocuses and other more modest plants. These daffodils and narcissi were planted in large groups of one kind, which is less fussy

than a mixture. They were selected (before the First World War), not only to cover a long season, starting with 'Princeps' in March and ending with the pheasant's eyes, *Narcissus poeticus* 'Recurvus', in May, but so that areas of white should alternate with others of yellow.

Mixed Borders

Dixter's is a high maintenance garden; I make no bones about that. It is effort that brings reward. There are many borders and much work goes into them. Labour saving ground cover is not for me. If you see ground cover, it's there because, first and foremost, I like it. If it does also save labour, that is an incidental benefit.

The borders are mixed, not herbaceous. I see no point in segregating plants of differing habit or habits. They can all help one another. So you'll see shrubs, climbers, hardy and tender perennials, annuals and biennials, all growing together and contributing to the overall tapestry.

Colour

I have no segregated colour schemes. In fact, I take it as a challenge to combine every sort of colour effectively. I have a constant awareness of colour and of what I am doing, but if I think a yellow candelabrum of mullein will look good rising from the middle of a quilt of pink phlox, I'll put it there – or let it put itself there. Many plants in this garden are self-sown and they often provide me with excellent ideas. But I do also have some of my own!

Fergus Garrett and I work hand in glove and he is as fertile in making suggestions for change and improvement as I am; so there is a continuing and productive exchange. Fergus is exceptionally energetic and inspiring, so a great deal gets done. Garden staff varies from five in winter to six in summer. This includes nursery work. They are a wonderfully supportive team. It would be impossible to exaggerate what a difference that makes, in so many ways.

Annuals and Bedding

Annuals and tender bedding plants feature prominently throughout the gardens, but they are not often seen in obvious beds of their own

Barn Garden and Sunk Garden in spring

them, in late summer, with michaelmas daisies or Korean chrysanthemums or other perennials that have been growing on in rows. Back-up areas are most important for gardening of this kind.

The Wall Garden
A rectangle of walls which cause destructive wind eddies and vortices. The protection they afford is largely in the imagination. The central rectangular lawn was replaced by paving, in 1998, which includes a pebble mosaic of my two dachshunds, Dahlia and Canna. The work was executed by Maggie Howarth and her assistant, Mark Davidson. The design was Miles Johnson's, a family Friend. The stones comprising Canna's eye and nose were given to me from the late Derek Jarman's highly original garden at Prospect Cottage, Dungeness.

and cut off from other features. For example, the largest single area of bedding, next to the old bay tree and facing the front of the house, is backed by a swathe of white Japanese anemones. They flower from late July to mid-October and provide a suitable background for any coloured bedding I choose to plant in front of them, and this varies with every year. Bedding allows you the swiftest opportunities for experiment and, if it goes wrong, the defects can quickly be obliterated.

This bedding is changed twice or even three times a year. Summer flowering annuals may not last the season through, so we often replace

Barn Garden and Sunk Garden
The Sunk Garden is surrounded by the Barn Garden. The floor of the Sunk Garden is largely carpeted with a low mat of the New Zealand *Acaena novae-zelandiae*, whose developing burrs are bright carmine, in July, in contrast to the yellow flowers of self-sown bird's foot trefoil (*Lotus corniculatus*). But about half of this floor is deliberately kept clear of plants, by the use of herbicides, which also keep the paving cracks elsewhere weed-free, without the necessity of lifting the slabs, as we once had to.

Some vertical contrast is good, in a flat area. In the pond itself, we are using *Canna glauca* for this purpose, while in the paving there is the giant reed grass, *Arundo donax*.

The Barn Garden has the merit of giving a good view across it wherever you may be standing. Visitors sometimes say 'If I could have just one bit of your garden, it would be this'. But that leaves out the need for a back-up area to feed into it.

The fig trees against the far barn wall were a Lutyens touch which you meet on other properties where he worked. They are there for foliage effect and he used the many-fingered Brunswick fig as being one of the most decorative. The gardens are a veritable bird sanctuary, rich in suitable nesting sites for many species and the blackbirds are particular favourites, so it is no use being cross with them for enjoying fruit. Neither do I mind the magpies; they prevent a population explosion among the smaller birds. Green woodpeckers are a common sight.

Barn Garden – Hydrangea 'Ayesha' and Buddleia 'Dartmoor'

The Garden's West Boundaries

Retracing through the Wall Garden, you emerge through Lutyens' second brick archway and should note his use of tiles, set on edge, in the paving at the start of his double flight of steps, the first, curved, the second, angled. Topiary yew 'coffee pots' are close to high hedges of olive green holm oak, commonly

Barn Garden – grasses, dahlias and cannas extending the season

No colour inhibitions; the Long Border in August

called ilex, *Quercus ilex*. There is a gap in this where I allowed an over-vigorous rambler rose to kill off a couple of oaks. When opened up, I liked the view of the twisted trunks of a crab, *Malus floribunda*, so much, that I have left this open, underplanting the crab with a carpet of *Epimedium pinnatum colchicum*. We strim over its tired old leaves, early in the year, and it then has bright yellow flowers among the coppery young foliage.

A closely planted strip of ash trees on the garden's west boundary, provide wonderful silhouettes of airy foliage against the sunset sky, in summer, but they do shed much seed into the garden, borne on the prevailing south-west winds.

From the bottom corner of the Topiary Garden, close to the Nursery entrance, there is a good view back to the house. This includes a piece of drained moat, shaped like a bath. It was here that my mother first practised her meadow gardening, and it still contains polyanthus plants from more than 70 years ago. There is also a large patch of snowflakes, *Leucojum aestivum*, and the largest colony of *Orchis mascula*.

The Exotic Garden

You can walk through the 'hovel', an old cow shed, on to the site of a one-time cattle yard (with their drinking tank in the centre), where Lutyens designed a formal rose garden. Thanks to replant disease, newly planted rose replacements ceased to thrive here, so on Fergus's arrival at Dixter, we made a grand alteration, got rid of the roses and created a late summer to autumn garden for tropical effect, though many of the best foliage plants are quite hardy. This has been a lot of fun. For colour, we are mainly using dahlias and cannas. There is a haze of purple from self-sowing *Verbena bonariensis*. A white, August–September flowering shrub, *Escallonia bifida*, is usually besieged by butterflies. The banana, *Musa basjoo*, is a hardy Japanese species.

The Long Border

Rising by way of Lutyens' circular steps, you reach a platform, on which were originally planted a pair of black mulberries, *Morus nigra*. Only one now remains and that was mutilated in the 1987 storm, but has made much new growth. The pair became too large for their site, so I did not replace the other, after that broke up in an earlier gale. Against the house wall, here, is an apricot, planted soon after the restorations. It fruits prodigiously in some years.

We are now at the bottom of the main section of the Long Border. Note the effective arrangement whereby it is separated from the informality of the orchard meadow, by a flagstone path, broad enough to allow of plants flowing onto it, and by a strip of mown grass. The orchard itself also has mown paths running through it. They not only allow access to its various parts but also indicate that the pervading roughness of the July scene is no accident. Lutyens' seat designs at the top of the Long Border, and in the Topiary Garden, have been twice replicated when renewal became necessary. Their simplicity reflects the timber structure of the house itself.

The border's season of interest is principally aimed at a mid-June to mid-August period, but in fact extends, albeit to a lesser degree at each end, from April to October. It is my belief that no gaps, showing bare earth, should be visible from late May on, apart from the most recent replacement plantings. The effect should be of a closely woven tapestry. I do not at all mind bringing some tall plants to the border's front, so long as an open texture allows the eye to see past them. Conversely, channels of low growth can be allowed, at times, to run to the back of the border.

For all the work that goes into it, I want the border to look exuberant and uncontrived. Self-sowers, like verbascums and *Verbena bonariensis*, help towards this.

The High Garden

A yew archway takes you out of the Long Border and through a passage garden, up to the High Garden. Look towards the house as you walk up the steps. There is a nice echo between the shapes of buildings in the background, and the architectural forms of yew topiary and hedges, in

An early summer display with pink and yellow lupins

front. These I have softened by planting in front of them a graceful bamboo, *Phyllostachys nigra.*

The High Garden was of a pattern typical of kitchen gardens in Edwardian times. Paths are flanked by fairly narrow flower borders, these being backed by espalier fruit trees which cut off the view of vegetable plots behind. I still grow a lot of vegetables, but nursery and garden stock is also assembled here.

The paths form a cross, with a central arena which used to be surrounded by anaemic pink hydrangeas ('Mme. Riverain'). I have replaced these with bolder shrubs, quite a number of them, conifers. The borders are otherwise the usual Lloyd mix, but with some emphasis on early summer, oriental poppies and lupins, prominent.

Completing the Circuit

There is a choice of routes, from the centre of the High Garden, but to complete the circuit,

you will make for another yew archway, leading to a garden containing 18 topiary birds. Originally intended as pheasants, fighting cocks, blackbirds and suchlike, we nowadays refer to them all as peacocks. There is a central platform around which the topiary is thickest; my mother referred to it as a parliament of birds or as a conversation piece.

The topiary used to be linked by double hedges of lavender, but lavender hates our heavy clay soil and constantly dies out, leaving unpluggable gaps. So I replaced, some 20 years ago, with hedges of an old michaelmas daisy that was in the garden from the first, *Aster lateriflorus* 'Horizontalis'. Not much above 2 ft tall, it has a sturdy, almost shrub-like habit, seething with white and purplish blossom in autumn and retaining a good shape till March, when we cut it down. The double rows are planted along the centre with an indigo blue 'English' iris, *I. latifolia*, which flowers at the turn of June-July.

A stock-bed planting in the High Garden

Garden Plan of Great Dixter

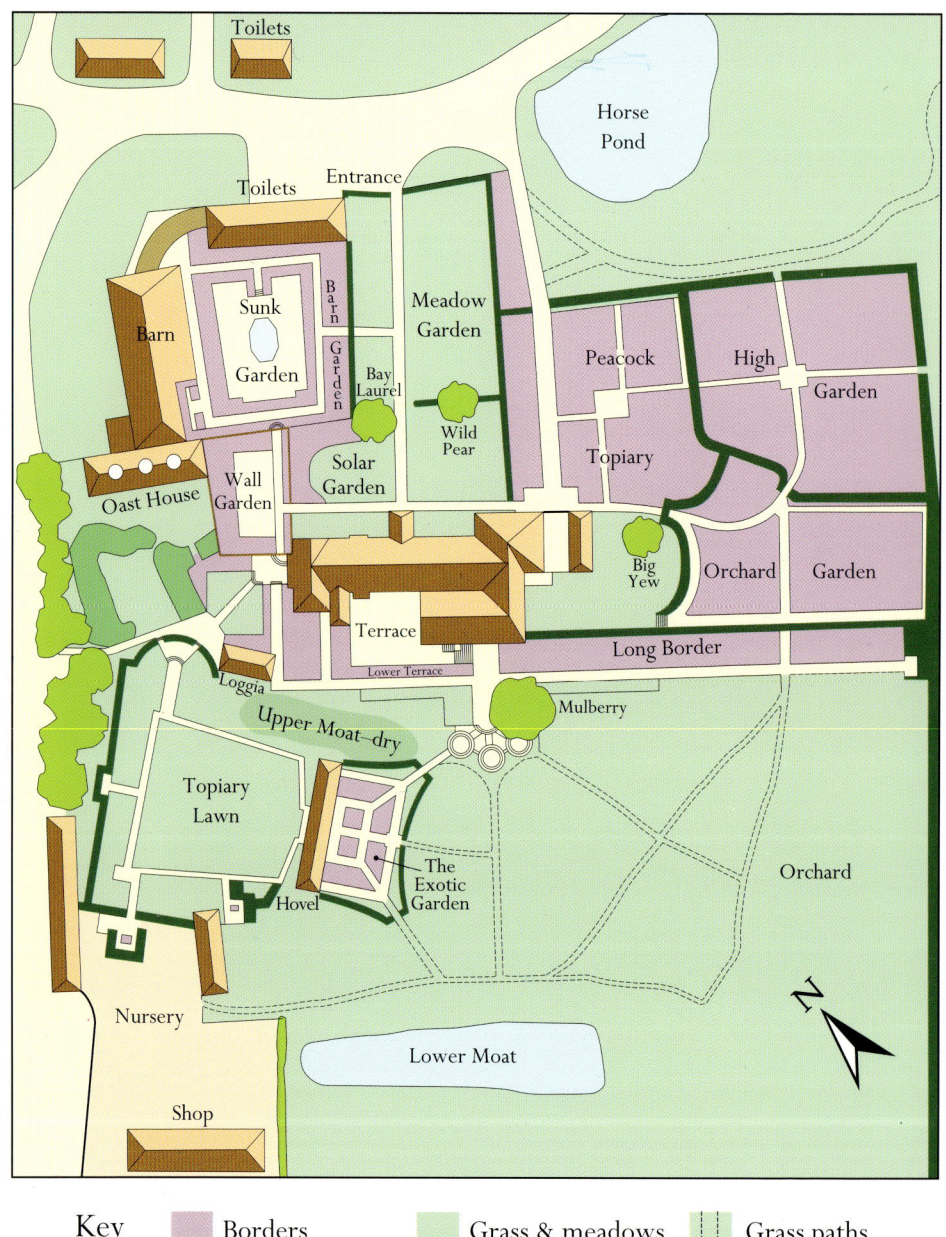

Toilets

Horse Pond

Toilets

Entrance

Barn

Sunk Garden

Barn Garden

Meadow Garden

Bay Laurel

Wild Pear

Peacock

High Garden

Topiary

Oast House

Wall Garden

Solar Garden

Big Yew

Orchard Garden

Terrace

Lower Terrace

Long Border

Loggia

Upper Moat—dry

Mulberry

Topiary Lawn

The Exotic Garden

Hovel

Orchard

Nursery

Lower Moat

Shop

Key

Borders

Grass & meadows

Grass paths

Yew hedges

Ilex hedge

Paved areas

Overleaf: The Long Border
Back cover: The Sunk Garden in February

Labels

The plants at Dixter are unlabelled. I know this is a bore, when you quickly want a plant's name. Generally there is someone to ask. Here are some of the reasons for my not labelling:

1. This is my own, personal garden; I do not have the obligations of an institution like a botanic or National Trust garden.
2. I hate the look of labels. Like a cemetery.
3. They are expensive in terms both of materials and the time needed to list the plants and to write and place the labels.
4. Plants (as against shrubs) need labels that are stuck into the ground. The public removes them, the more easily to read, but does not replace them firmly or even in the right place.
5. It is easier to pop a label into a handbag than to try and memorise it on the spot.
6. The wrong label is read for the name of the plant to be identified.
7. Visitors dart into the border, oblivious of footprints, the better to read a label that is out of reach from the front.
8. If all labels are for that reason placed at the front, misapplication of names will be aggravated.
9. Even when plants are clearly labelled, the public will still ask their name if anyone is around to talk to. They're on an outing. We're trying to work.

Sorry!

Christopher Lloyd

Great Dixter Nurseries

The Nursery is to be found just below the Topiary Lawn. A large number of the plants seen growing throughout the gardens are available for you to take home and try for yourself. Clematis *are* a speciality but we also offer a large range of plantsmen's plants.

Staffed by keen, knowledgeable gardeners even the most timid horticultural novice should not be reticent about asking for advice. "The bright red thing at the far end of the Barn Garden" is usually sufficient information to ensure you identify your plant.

Nursery Opening Hours

April to October   Daily (including Sundays)
                         9.00–12.30 and 1.30–5.00
October to April   Weekdays
                         9.00–12.30 and 1.30–5.00
                         Saturdays
                         9.00–12.30

Plants are also available by mail order.
Please either purchase a catalogue at the Nursery or send 4 First Class stamps to:
Great Dixter Nurseries, Northiam, Rye, East Sussex TN31 6PH.

All Nursery enquiries on 01797 253107

A foggy autumn morning in the Exotic Garden

ISBN 0-9525471-0-4